Data science from scratch

Intermediate guide for learning Data science and master it like a pro(Comprehensive guide)

TABLE OF CONTENTS

It's in all of us. Data science is what makes us humans what we are today. No, not the computer-driven data science this book will introduce you to, but the ability of our brains to see connections, draw conclusions from facts, and learn from our past experiences. More so than any other species on the planet, we depend on our brains for survival; we went all-in on these features to earn our place in nature. That strategy has worked out for us so far, and we're unlikely to change it in the near future.

But our brains can only take us so far when it comes to raw computing. Our biology can't keep up with the amounts of data we can capture now and with the extent of our curiosity. So we turn to machines to do part of the work for us: to recognize patterns, create connections, and supply us with answers to our numerous questions.

The quest for knowledge is in our genes. Relying on computers to do part of the job for us is not—but it is our destiny.

INTRODUCTION

There's a joke that says a data scientist is someone who knows more statistics than a computer scientist and more computer science than a statistician. (I didn't say it was a good joke.) In fact, some data scientists are — for all practical purposes — statisticians, while others are pretty much indistinguishable from software engineers. Some are machine-learning experts, while others couldn't machine-learn their way out of kindergarten. Some are PhDs with impressive publication records, while others have never read an academic paper (shame on them, though). In short, pretty much no matter how you define data science, you'll find practitioners for whom the definition is totally, absolutely wrong.

Nonetheless, we won't let that stop us from trying. We'll say that a data scientist is someone who extracts insights from messy data. Today's world is full of people trying to turn data into insight.

For instance, the dating site OkCupid asks its members to answer thousands of questions in order to find the most appropriate matches for them. But it also analyzes these results to figure out innocuous-sounding questions you can ask someone to find out how likely someone is to sleep with you on the first date.

Facebook asks you to list your hometown and your current location, ostensibly to make it easier for your friends to find and connect with you. But it also analyzes these locations to identify global migration patterns and where the fanbases of different football teams live.

As a large retailer, Target tracks your purchases and interactions, both online and in-store. And it uses the data to predictively model which of its customers are pregnant, to better market baby-related purchases to them.

In 2012, the Obama campaign employed dozens of data scientists who data-mined and experimented their way to identifying voters who needed extra attention, choosing optimal donor-specific fundraising appeals and programs, and focusing get-out-the-vote efforts where they were most likely to be useful. It is generally agreed that these efforts played an important role in the president's re-election, which means it is a safe bet that political campaigns of the future will become more and more data-driven, resulting in a never ending arms race of data science and data collection.

Now, before you start feeling too jaded: some data scientists also occasionally use their skills for good — using data to make government more effective, to help the homeless, and to improve public health. But it certainly won't hurt your career if you like figuring out the best way to get people to click on advertisements.

CHAPTER 1

Getting started on Your Data Science Toolbox

The distribution of GNU/ Linux that we are using, Ubuntu, comes with a whole bunch of command-line tools pre-installed. Moreover, Ubuntu offers many packages that contain other, relevant command-line tools. Installing these packages yourself is not too difficult. However, we also use command-line tools that are not available as packages and require a more manual, and more involved, installation. In order to acquire the necessary command line tools without having to go through the involved installation process of each, we encourage you to install the Data Science Toolbox.

The Data Science Toolbox is a virtual environment that allows you to get started doing data science in minutes. The default version comes with commonly used soft- ware for data science, including the Python scientific stack and R together with its most popular packages. Additional software and data bundles are easily installed. These bundles can be specific to a certain book, course, or organization. You can read more about the Data Science Toolbox at its website.

There are two ways to set up the Data Science Toolbox:

(1) installing it locally using VirtualBox and Vagrant or

(2) launching it in the cloud using Amazon Web Services.

Both ways result in exactly the same environment. In this chapter, we explain how to set up the Data Science Toolbox for Data Science at the Command Line locally.

The easiest way to install the Data Science Toolbox is on your local machine. Because the local version of the Data Science Toolbox runs on top of VirtualBox and Vagrant, it can be installed on Linux, Mac OS X, and Microsoft Windows.

Step 1: Download and Install VirtualBox

Browse to the VirtualBox (Oracle, 2014) download page and download the appropriate binary for your operating system. Open the binary and follow the installation instructions.

Step 2: Download and Install Vagrant

Similar to Step 1, browse to the Vagrant (HashiCorp, 2014) download page and download the appropriate binary. Open the binary and follow the installation instructions. If you already have Vagrant installed, please make sure that it's version 1.5 or higher.

Step 3: Download and Start the Data Science Toolbox

Open a terminal (known as the Command Prompt or PowerShell in Microsoft Windows). Create a directory, e.g., MyDataScienceToolbox, and navigate to it by typing:

- $ mkdir MyDataScienceToolbox

- $ cd MyDataScienceToolbox

In order to initialize the Data Science Toolbox, run the following command:

- $ vagrant init data-science-toolbox/data-science-at-the-command-line

This creates a file named Vagrantfile. This is a configuration file that tells Vagrant how to launch the virtual machine. This file contains a lot of lines that are commented out.

Example. Minimal configuration for Vagrant

Vagrant.configure(2) do |config|

config.vm.box = "data-science-toolbox/data-science-at-the-command-line"
end

By running the following command, the Data Science Toolbox will be downloaded and booted:

- $ vagrant up

If everything went well, then you now have a Data Science Toolbox running on your local machine.

If you ever see the message default: Warning: Connection time out. Retrying... printed repeatedly, then it may be that the virtual machine is waiting for input. This may happen when the virtual machine has not been properly shut down. In order to find out what's wrong, add the following lines to Vagrantfile before the last end statement:

config.vm.provider "virtualbox" do |vb|

vb.gui = true

end

This will cause VirtualBox to show a screen. Once the virtual machine has booted and you have identified the problem, you can remove these lines from Vagrantfile. The username and password to log in are both vagrant. If this doesn't help, we advise you to check the book's website, as this website contains an up-to-date list of frequently asked questions.

Below Example shows a slightly more elaborate Vagrantfile. You can view more configuration options at http://docs.vagrantup.com.

Example - *Configuring Vagrant*

Vagrant.require_version ">= 1.5.0"

Vagrant.configure(2) do |config|

config.vm.box = "data-science-toolbox/data-science-at-the-command-line"

config.vm.network "forwarded_port", guest: 8000, host: 8000

config.vm.provider "virtualbox" do |vb|

vb.gui = true

vb.memory = 2048

vb.cpus = 2

end

end

- Require at least version of Vagrant.

- Forward port 8000. This is useful if you want to view a figure you created.

- Launch a graphical user interface.

- Use 2 GB of memory.

- Use 2 CPUs.

Step 4: Log In (on Linux and Mac OS X)

If you are running Linux, Mac OS X, or some other Unix-like operating system, you can log in to the Data Science Toolbox by running the following command in a terminal:

- $ vagrant ssh

After a few seconds, you will be greeted with the following message:

Welcome to the Data Science Toolbox for Data Science at the Command Line

Based on Ubuntu 14.04 LTS (GNU/Linux 3.13.0-24-generic x86_64)

- Data Science at the Command Line: http://datascienceatthecommandline.com

- Data Science Toolbox: http://datasciencetoolbox.org

- Ubuntu documentation: http://help.ubuntu.com

Last login: Tue Jul 22 19:33:16 2014 from 10.0.2.2

Step 4: Log In (on Microsoft Windows)

If you are running Microsoft Windows, you need to either run Vagrant with a graphical user interface (refer back to Step 2 on how to set that up) or use a third-party application in order to log in to the Data Science Toolbox. For the latter, we recommend PuTTY. Browse to the PuTTY download page and download putty.exe. Run PuTTY, and enter the following values:

- Host Name (or IP address): 127.0.0.1

- Port: 2222

- Connection type: SSH

If you want, you can save these values as a session by clicking the Save button, so that you do not need to enter these values again. Click the Open button and enter vagrant for both the username and the password.

Step 5: Shut Down or Start Anew

The Data Science Toolbox can be shut down by running the following command from the same directory as you ran vagrant up:

- $ vagrant halt

In case you wish to get rid of the Data Science Toolbox and start over, you can type:

- $ vagrant destroy

Then, return to the instructions for Step 3 to set up the Data Science Toolbox again.

CHAPTER 2

Applications For Machine Learning In Data Science

Regression and classification are of primary importance to a data scientist. To achieve these goals, one of the main tools a data scientist uses is machine learning. The uses for regression and automatic classification are wide ranging, such as the following:

• Finding oil fields, gold mines, or archeological sites based on existing sites (classification and regression)

• Finding place names or persons in text (classification)

• Identifying people based on pictures or voice recordings (classification)

• Recognizing birds based on their whistle (classification)

• Identifying profitable customers (regression and classification)

• Proactively identifying car parts that are likely to fail (regression)

• Identifying tumors and diseases (classification)

- Predicting the amount of money a person will spend on product X (regression)

- Predicting the number of eruptions of a volcano in a period (regression)

- Predicting your company's yearly revenue (regression)

- Predicting which team will win the Champions League in soccer (classification)

Occasionally data scientists build a model (an abstraction of reality) that provides insight to the underlying processes of a phenomenon. When the goal of a model isn't prediction but interpretation, it's called root cause analysis. Here are a few examples:

- Understanding and optimizing a business process, such as determining which products add value to a product line

- Discovering what causes diabetes

- Determining the causes of traffic jams

This list of machine learning applications can only be seen as an appetizer because it's ubiquitous within data science. Regression and classification are two important techniques, but the repertoire and the applications don't end, with clustering as one other example of a valuable technique. Machine learning techniques can be used throughout the data science process, as we'll discuss in the next section.

Where machine learning is used in the data science process

Although machine learning is mainly linked to the data-modeling step of the data science process, it can be used at almost every step.

The data modeling phase can't start until you have qualitative raw data you can understand. But prior to that, the data preparation phase can benefit from the use of machine learning. An example would be cleansing a list of text strings; machine learning can group similar strings together so it becomes easier to correct spelling errors.

Machine learning is also useful when exploring data. Algorithms can root out underlying patterns in the data where they'd be difficult to find with only charts.

Given that machine learning is useful throughout the data science process, it shouldn't come as a surprise that a considerable number of Python libraries were developed to make your life a bit easier.

Python tools used in machine learning

Python has an overwhelming number of packages that can be used in a machine learning setting. The Python machine learning ecosystem can be divided into three main types of packages.

Packages For Working With Data In Memory

When prototyping, the following packages can get you started by providing advanced functionalities with a few lines of code:

• SciPy is a library that integrates fundamental packages often used in scientific computing such as NumPy, matplotlib, Pandas, and SymPy.

- NumPy gives you access to powerful array functions and linear algebra functions.

- Matplotlib is a popular 2D plotting package with some 3D functionality.

- Pandas is a high-performance, but easy-to-use, data-wrangling package. It introduces dataframes to Python, a type of in-memory data table. It's a concept that should sound familiar to regular users of R.

- SymPy is a package used for symbolic mathematics and computer algebra.

- StatsModels is a package for statistical methods and algorithms.

- Scikit-learn is a library filled with machine learning algorithms.

- RPy2 allows you to call R functions from within Python. R is a popular open source statistics program.

- NLTK (Natural Language Toolkit) is a Python toolkit with a focus on text analytics.

-

These libraries are good to get started with, but once you make the decision to run a certain Python program at frequent intervals, performance comes into play.

Optimizing operations

Once your application moves into production, the libraries listed here can help you deliver the speed you need. Sometimes this involves connecting to big data infrastructures such as Hadoop and Spark.

Numba and NumbaPro—These use just-in-time compilation to speed up applications written directly in Python and a few annotations. NumbaPro also allows you to use the power of your graphics processor unit (GPU).

PyCUDA—This allows you to write code that will be executed on the GPU instead of your CPU and is therefore ideal for calculation-heavy applications. It works best with problems that lend themselves to being parallelized and need little input compared to the number of required computing cycles. An example is studying the robustness of your predictions by calculating thousands of different outcomes based on a single start state.

Cython, or C for Python—This brings the C programming language to Python. C is a lower-level language, so the code is closer to what the computer eventually uses (bytecode). The closer code is to bits and bytes, the faster it executes. A computer is also faster when it knows the type of a variable (called static typing). Python wasn't designed to do this, and Cython helps you to overcome this shortfall.

Blaze—Blaze gives you data structures that can be bigger than your computer's main memory, enabling you to work with large data sets.

Dispy and IPCluster—These packages allow you to write code that can be distributed over a cluster of computers.

PP—Python is executed as a single process by default. With the help of PP you can parallelize computations on a single machine or over clusters.

Pydoop and Hadoopy—These connect Python to Hadoop, a common big data framework.

PySpark—This connects Python and Spark, an in-memory big data framework.

Now that you've seen an overview of the available libraries, let's look at the modeling

process itself.

The modeling process

The modeling phase consists of four steps:

1 Feature engineering and model selection

2 Training the model

3 Model validation and selection

4 Applying the trained model to unseen data

Before you find a good model, you'll probably iterate among the first three steps.

The last step isn't always present because sometimes the goal isn't prediction but explanation (root cause analysis). For instance, you might want to find out the causes of species' extinctions but not necessarily predict which one is next in line to leave our planet.

It's possible to chain or combine multiple techniques. When you chain multiple models, the output of the first model becomes an input for the second model. When you combine multiple models, you train them independently and combine their results. This last technique is also known as ensemble learning.

A model consists of constructs of information called features or predictors and a target or response variable. Your model's goal is to predict the target variable, for example, tomorrow's high temperature. The variables that help you do this and are (usually) known to you are the features or predictor variables such as today's temperature, cloud movements, current wind speed, and so on. The best models are those that accurately represent reality, preferably while staying concise and interpretable. To achieve this, feature engineering is the most important and arguably most interesting part of modeling.

For example, an important feature in a model that tried to explain the extinction of large land animals in the last 60,000 years in Australia turned out to be the population number and spread of humans.

Engineering features and selecting a model

With engineering features, you must come up with and create possible predictors for the model. This is one of the most important steps in the process because a model recombines these features to achieve its predictions. Often you may need to consult an expert or the appropriate literature to come up with meaningful features.

Certain features are the variables you get from a data set, as is the case with the provided data sets in our exercises and in most school exercises. In practice you'll need to find the features yourself, which may be scattered among different data sets. In several projects we had to bring together more than 20 different data sources before we had the raw data we required. Often you'll need to apply a transformation to an input before it becomes a good predictor or to combine multiple inputs. An example of combining multiple inputs would be interaction variables: the impact of either single variable is low, but if both are present their impact becomes immense. This is especially true in chemical and medical environments. For example, although vinegar and bleach are fairly harmless common household products by themselves, mixing them results in poisonous chlorine gas, a gas that killed thousands during World War I.

In medicine, clinical pharmacy is a discipline dedicated to researching the effect of the interaction of medicines. This is an important job, and it doesn't even have to involve two medicines to produce potentially dangerous results. For example, mixing an antifungal medicine such as Sporanox with grapefruit has serious side effects.

Sometimes you have to use modeling techniques to derive features: the output of a model becomes part of another model. This isn't uncommon, especially in text mining.

Documents can first be annotated to classify the content into categories, or you can count the number of geographic places or persons in the text. This counting is often more difficult than it sounds; models are first applied to recognize certain words as a person or a place. All this new information is then poured into the model you want to build. One of the biggest mistakes in model construction is the availability bias:

your features are only the ones that you could easily get your hands on and your model consequently represents this one-sided "truth." Models suffering from availability bias often fail when they're validated because it becomes clear that they're not a valid representation of the truth.

In World War II, after bombing runs on German territory, many of the English planes came back with bullet holes in the wings, around the nose, and near the tail of the plane. Almost none of them had bullet holes in the cockpit, tail rudder, or engine block, so engineering decided extra armor plating should be added to the wings. This looked like a sound idea until a mathematician by the name of Abraham Wald explained the obviousness of their mistake: they only took into account the planes that returned. The bullet holes on the wings were actually the least of their concern, because at least a plane with this kind of damage could make it back home for repairs.

Plane fortification was hence increased on the spots that were unscathed on returning planes. The initial reasoning suffered from availability bias: the engineers ignored an important part of the data because it was harder to obtain. In this case they were lucky, because the reasoning could be reversed to get the intended result without getting the data from the crashed planes.

When the initial features are created, a model can be trained to the data.

CHAPTER 3

Identifying Data Problems

Data Science is different from other areas such as mathematics of statistics. Data Science is an applied activity and data scientists serve the needs and solve the problems of data users. Before you can solve a problem, you need to identify it and this process is not always as obvious as it might seem. In this chapter, we discuss the identification of data problems.

Apple farmers live in constant fear, first for their blossoms and later for their fruit. A late spring frost can kill the blossoms. Hail or extreme wind in the summer can damage the fruit. More generally, farming is an activity that is first and foremost in the physical world, with complex natural processes and forces, like weather, that are beyond the control of humankind.

In this highly physical world of unpredictable natural forces, is there any role for data science? On the surface there does not seem to be. But how can we know for sure? Having a nose for identifying data problems requires openness, curiosity, creativity, and a willingness to ask a lot of questions. In fact, the impression that a data scientist sits in front a of computer all day and works a crazy program like R, that is a mistake.

Every data scientist must (eventually) become immersed in the problem domain where she is working. The data scientist may never actually become a farmer, but if you are going to identify a data problem that a farmer has, you have to learn to think like a farmer, to some degree.

To get this domain knowledge you can read or watch videos, but the best way is to ask "subject matter experts" (in this case farmers) about what they do. The whole process of asking questions deserves its own treatment, but for now there are three things to think about when asking questions. First, you want the subject matter experts, or SMEs, as they are sometimes called, to tell stories of what they do. Then you want to ask them about anomalies: the unusual things that happen for better or for worse. Finally, you want to ask about risks and uncertainty: what are the situations where it is hard to tell what will happen next - and what happens next could have a profound effect on whether the situation ends badly or well. Each of these three areas of questioning reflects an approach to identifying data problems that may turn up something good that could be accomplished with data, information, and the right decision at the right time.

The purpose of asking about stories is that people mainly think in stories. From farmers to teachers to managers to CEOs, people know and tell stories about success and failure in their particular domain. Stories are powerful ways of communicating wisdom between different members of the same profession and they are ways of collecting a sense of identity that sets one profession apart from another profession. The only problem is that stories can be wrong.

If you can get a professional to tell the main stories that guide how she conducts her work, you can then consider how to verify that story. Without questioning the veracity of the person that tells the story, you can imagine ways of measuring the different aspects of how things happen in the story with an eye towards eventually verifying (or sometimes debunking) the stories that guide professional work.

For example, the farmer might say that in the deep spring frost that occurred five years ago, the trees in the hollow were spared frost damage while the trees around the ridge of the hill had more damage. For this reason, on a cold night the farmer places most of the smudgepots (containers that hold a fuel that creates a smoky fire) around the ridge. The farmer strongly believes that this strategy works, but does it? It would be possible to collect time-series temperature data from multiple locations within the orchard on cold and warm nights, and on nights with and without smudgepots.

The data could be used to create a model of temperature changes in the different areas of the orchard and this model could support, improve, or debunk the story.

A second strategy for problem identification is to look for the exception cases, both good and bad. A little later in the book we will learn about how the core of classic methods of statistical inference is to characterize "the center" - the most typical cases that occur - and then examine the extreme cases that are far from the center for information that could help us understand an intervention or an unusual combination of circumstances. Identifying unusual cases is a powerful way of understanding how things work, but it is necessary first to define the central or most typical occurrences in order to have an accurate idea of what constitutes an unusual case.

Coming back to our farmer friend, in advance of a thunderstorm late last summer, a powerful wind came through the orchard, tearing the fruit off the trees. Most of the trees lost a small amount of fruit: the dropped apples could be seen near the base of the tree.

One small grouping of trees seemed to lose a much larger amount of fruit, however, and the drops were apparently scattered much further from the trees. Is it possible that some strange wind conditions made the situation worse in this one spot? Or is just a matter of chance that a few trees in the same area all lost a bit more fruit than would be typical.

A systematic count of lost fruit underneath a random sample of trees would help to answer this question. The bulk of the trees would probably have each lost about the same amount, but more importantly, that "typical" group would give us a yardstick against which we could determine what would really count as unusual.

When we found an unusual set of cases that was truly beyond the limits of typical, we could rightly focus our attention on these to try to understand the anomaly.

A third strategy for identifying data problems is to find out about risk and uncertainty. If you read the previous chapter you may remember that a basic function of information is to reduce uncertainty.

It is often valuable to reduce uncertainty because of how risk affects the things we all do. At work, at school, at home, life is full of risks: making a decision or failing to do so sets off a chain of events that may lead to something good or something not so good.

It is difficult to say, but in general we would like to narrow things down in a way that maximizes the chances of a good outcome and minimizes the chance of a bad one. To do this, we need to make better decisions and to make better decisions we need to reduce uncertainty.

By asking questions about risks and uncertainty (and decisions) a data scientist can zero in on the problems that matter. You can even look at the previous two strategies - asking about the stories that comprise professional wisdom and asking about anomalies/unusual cases - in terms of the potential for reducing uncertainty and risk.

In the case of the farmer, much of the risk comes from the weather, and the uncertainty revolves around which countermeasures will be cost effective under prevailing conditions. Consuming lots of expensive oil in smudgepots on a night that turns out to be quite warm is a waste of resources that could make the difference between a profitable or an unprofitable year. So more precise and timely information about local weather conditions might be a key focus area for problem solving with data. What if a live stream of national weather service doppler radar could appear on the farmer's smart phone? Let's build an app for that...

CHAPTER 4

Introducing Connected Data And Graph Databases

Let's start by familiarizing ourselves with the concept of connected data and its representation as graph data.

Connected data – As the name indicates, connected data is characterized by the fact that the data at hand has a relationship that makes it connected.

Graphs – Often referred to in the same sentence as connected data. Graphs are well suited to represent the connectivity of data in a meaningful way.

Graph databases – The reason this subject is meriting particular attention is because, besides the fact that data is increasing in size, it's also becoming more interconnected. Not much effort is needed to come up with well-known examples of connected data.

A prominent example of data that takes a network form is social media data. Social media allows us to share and exchange data in networks, thereby generating a great amount of connected data. We can illustrate this with a simple example. Let's assume we have two people in our data,

User1 and User2. Furthermore, we know the first name and the last name of User1 (first name: Paul and last name: Beun) and User2 (first name: Jelme and last name: Ragnar). A natural way of representing this could be by drawing it out on a whiteboard.

Entities — We have two entities that represent people (User1 and User2). These entities have the properties "name" and "lastname".

Properties — The properties are defined by key-value pairs. From this graph we can also infer that User1 with the "name" property Paul knows User2 with the "name" property Jelme.

Relationships — This is the relationship between Paul and Jelme. Note that the relationship has a direction: it's Paul who "knows" Jelme and not the other way around. User1 and User2 both represent people and could therefore be grouped.

Labels — In a graph database, one can group nodes by using labels. User1 and User2 could in this case both be labeled as "User".

Connected data often contains many more entities and connections.

Two more entities are included: Country1 with the name Cambodia and Country2 with the name Sweden. Two more relationships exist: "Has_been_in" and "Is_born_in". In the previous graph, only the entities included a property, now the relationships also contain a property. Such graphs are known as property graphs. The relationship connecting the nodes User1 and Country1 is of the type "Has_been_in" and has as a property "Date" which represents a data value. Similarly, User2 is connected to Country2 but through a different type of relationship, which is of the type "Is_born_in". Note that the types of relationships provide us a context of the relationships between nodes. Nodes can have multiple relationships.

This kind of representation of our data gives us an intuitive way to store connected data. To explore our data we need to traverse through the graph following predefined paths to find the patterns we're searching for. What if one would like to know where Paul has been? Translated into graph database terminology, we'd like to find the pattern "Paul has been in." To answer this, we'd start at the node with the name "Paul" and traverse to

Cambodia via the relationship "Has_been_in". Hence a graph traversal, which corresponds to a database query, would be the following:

1 A starting node — In this case the node with name property "Paul"

2 A traversal path — In this case a path starting at node Paul and going to Cambodia

3 End node — Country node with name property "Cambodia"

To better understand how graph databases deal with connected data, it's appropriate to expand a bit more on graphs in general. Graphs are extensively studied in the domains of computer science and mathematics in a field called graph theory. Graph theory is the study of graphs, where graphs represent the mathematical structures used to model pairwise relations between objects. What makes them so appealing is that they have a structure that lends itself to visualizing connected data. A graph is defined by vertices (also known as nodes in the graph database world) and edges (also known as relationships). These concepts form the basic fundamentals on which graph data structures are based.

Compared to other data structures, a distinctive feature of connected data is its nonlinear nature: any entity can be connected to any other via a variety of relationship types and intermediate entities and paths. In graphs, you can make a subdivision between directed and undirected graphs. The edges of a directed graph have — how could it be otherwise — a direction. Although one could argue that every problem could somehow be represented as a graph problem, it's important to understand when it's ideal to do so and when it's not.

Why and when should I use a graph database?

The quest of determining which graph database one should use could be an involved process to undertake. One important aspect in this decision making process is finding the right representation for your data. Since the early 1970s the most common type of database one had to rely on was a relational one. Later, others emerged, such as the hierarchical database (for example, IMS), and the graph database's closest relative: the network database (for example, IDMS). But during the last decades the landscape has become much more diverse, giving end-users more choice depending on their specific needs. Considering the recent development of the data that's becoming available, two characteristics are well suited to be highlighted here.

The first one is the size of the data and the other the complexity of the data.

we'll need to rely on a graph database when the data is complex but still small. Though "small" is a relative thing here, we're still talking hundreds of millions of nodes. Handling complexity is the main asset of a graph database and the ultimate "why" you'd use it. To explain what kind of complexity is meant here, first think about how a traditional relational database works.

Contrary to what the name of relational databases indicates, not much is relational about them except that the foreign keys and primary keys are what relate tables. In contrast, relationships in graph databases are first-class citizens. Through this aspect, they lend themselves well to modeling and querying connected data. A relational database would rather strive for minimizing data redundancy. This process is known as database normalization, where a table is decomposed into smaller (less redundant) tables while maintaining all the information intact. In a normalized database one needs to conduct changes of an attribute in only one table. The aim of this process is to isolate data changes in one table. Relational database management systems (RDBMS) are a good choice as a database for data that fits nicely into a tabular format. The relationships in the data can be expressed by joining the tables. Their fit starts to downgrade when the joins become more complicated, especially when they become many-to-many joins. Query time will also increase when your data size starts increasing, and maintaining the database will be more of a challenge.

These factors will hamper the performance of your database. Graph databases, on the other hand, inherently store data as nodes and relationships. Although graph databases are classified as a NoSQL type of database, a trend to present them as a category in their own right exists. One seeks the justification for this by noting that the other types of NoSQL databases are aggregation-oriented, while graph databases aren't.

A relational database might, for example, have a table representing "people" and their properties. Any person is related to other people through kinship (and friendship, and so on); each row might represent a person, but connecting them to other rows in the people table would be an immensely difficult job. Do you add a variable that holds the unique identifier of the first child and an extra one to hold the ID of the second child? Where do you stop? Tenth child?

An alternative would be to use an intermediate table for child-parent relationships, but you'll need a separate one for other relationship types like friendship. In this last case you don't get column proliferation but table proliferation: one relationship table for each type of relationship. Even if you somehow succeed in modeling the data in such a way that all family relations are present, you'll need difficult queries to get the answer to simple questions such as "I would like the grandsons of John McBain." First you need to find John McBain's children. Once you find his children, you need to find theirs. By the time you have found all the grandsons, you have hit the "people" table three times:

1.   Find McBain and fetch his children.

2.   Look up the children with the IDs you got and get the IDs of their children.

3.   Find the grandsons of McBain.

Recursive lookups such as these are inefficient, to say the least.

CHAPTER 5

Analyst Perspective On Data Repositories

The introduction of spreadsheets enabled business users to create simple logic on data structured in rows and columns and create their own analyses of business problems. Database administrator training is not required to create spreadsheets: They can be set up to do many things quickly and independently of information technology (IT) groups. Spreadsheets are easy to share, and end users have control over the logic involved. However, their proliferation can result in "many versions of the truth." In other words, it can be challenging to determine if a particular user has the most relevant version of a spreadsheet, with the most current data and logic in it. Moreover, if a laptop is lost or a file becomes corrupted, the data and logic within the spreadsheet could be lost. This is an ongoing challenge because spreadsheet programs such as Microsoft Excel still run on many computers worldwide. With the proliferation of data islands (or spread marts), the need to centralize the data is more pressing than ever.

As data needs grew, so did more scalable data warehousing solutions. These technologies enabled data to be managed centrally, providing benefits of security, failover, and a single repository where users could rely on getting an "official" source of data for financial reporting or other mission-critical tasks. This structure also enabled the creation ofOLAP cubes and 81 analytical tools, which provided quick access to a set of dimensions within an RD8MS. More advanced features enabled performance of in-depth analytical techniques such as regressions and neural networks. Enterprise Data Warehouses (EDWs) are critical for reporting and 81 tasks and solve many of the problems that proliferating spreadsheets introduce, such as which of multiple versions of a spreadsheet is correct. EDWs-and a good 81 strategy-provide direct data feeds from sources that are centrally managed, backed up, and secured.

Despite the benefits of EDWs and 81, these systems tend to restrict the flexibility needed to perform robust or exploratory data analysis. With the EDW model, data is managed and controlled by IT groups and database administrators (D8As), and data analysts must depend on IT for access and changes to the data schemas. This imposes longer lead times for analysts to get data; most of the time is spent waiting for approvals rather than starting meaningful work. Additionally, many times the EDW rules restrict analysts from building datasets. Consequently, it is common for additional systems to emerge containing critical data for constructing analytic data sets, managed locally by power users. IT groups generally dislike existence of data sources outside of their control because, unlike an EDW, these data sets are not managed, secured, or backed up. From an analyst perspective, EDW and 81 solve problems related to data accuracy and availability. However, EDW and 81 introduce new problems related to flexibility and agility, which were less pronounced when dealing with spreadsheets.

A solution to this problem is the analytic sandbox, which attempts to resolve the conflict for analysts and data scientists with EDW and more formally managed corporate data. In this model, the IT group may still manage the analytic sandboxes, but they will be purposefully designed to enable robust analytics, while being centrally managed and secured. These sandboxes, often referred to as workspaces, are designed to enable teams to explore many datasets in a controlled fashion and are not typically used for enterpriselevel financial reporting and sales dashboards.

Many times, analytic sandboxes enable high-performance computing using in-database processing the analytics occur within the database itself. The idea is that performance of the analysis will be better if the analytics are run in the database itself, rather than bringing the data to an analytical tool that resides somewhere else. "Advanced Analytics- Technology and Tools: In-Database Analytics." creates relationships to multiple data sources within an organization and saves time spent creating these data feeds on an individual basis. In-database processing for deep analytics enables faster turnaround time for developing and executing new analytic models, while reducing, though not eliminating, the cost associated with data stored in local, "shadow" file systems. In addition, rather than the typical structured data in the EDW, analytic sandboxes can house a greater variety of data, such as raw data, textual data, and other kinds of unstructured data, without interfering with critical production databases.

There are several things to consider with Big Data Analytics projects to ensure the approach fits with the desired goals. Due to the characteristics of Big Data, these projects lend themselves to decision support for high-value, strategic decision making with high processing complexity. The analytic techniques used in this context need to be iterative and flexible, due to the high volume of data and its complexity.

Performing rapid and complex analysis requires high throughput network connections and a consideration for the acceptable amount of latency. For instance, developing a real-time product recommender for a website imposes greater system demands than developing a near real time recommender, which may still provide acceptable performance, have sl ightly greater latency, and may be cheaper to deploy. These considerations require a different approach to thinking about analytics challenges, which will be explored further in the next section.

BI Versus Data Science

The four business drivers require a variety of analytical techniques to address them properly. Although much is written generally about analytics, it is important to distinguish between Bland Data Science. There are several ways to compare these groups of analytical techniques.

One way to evaluate the type of analysis being performed is to examine the time horizon and the kind of analytical approaches being used. BI tends to provide reports, dashboards, and queries on business questions for the current period or in the past. BI systems make it easy to answer questions related to quarter-to-date revenue, progress toward quarterly targets, and understand how much of a given product was sold in a prior quarter or year. These questions tend to be closed-ended and explain current or past behavior, typically by aggregating historical data and grouping it in some way. BI provides hindsight and some insight and generally answers questions related to "when" and "where" events occurred.

By comparison, Data Science tends to use disaggregated data in a more forward-looking, exploratory way, focusing on analyzing the present and enabling informed decisions about the future. Rather than aggregating historical data to look at how many of a given product sold in the previous quarter, a team may employ Data Science techniques such as time series analysis.

Analytical Theory and Methods: Time Series Analysis," to forecast future product sales and revenue more accurately than extending a simple trend line. In addition, Data Science tends to be more exploratory in nature and may use scenario optimization to deal with more open-ended questions. This approach provides insight into current activity and foresight into future events, while generally focusing on questions related to "how" and "why" events occur.

Where BI problems tend to require highly structured data organized in rows and columns for accurate reporting, Data Science projects tend to use many types of data sources, including large or unconventional datasets. Depending on an organization's goals, it may choose to embark on a BI project if it is doing reporting, creating dashboards, or performing simple visualizations, or it may choose Data Science projects if it needs to do a more sophisticated analysis with disaggregated or varied datasets.

CHAPTER 6

Emerging Big Data Ecosystem And A New Approach To Analytics

Organizations and data collectors are realizing that the data they can gather from individuals contains intrinsic value and, as a result, a new economy is emerging. As this new digital economy continues to evolve, the market sees the introduction of data vendors and data cleaners that use crowdsourcing (such as Mechanical Turk and Ga laxyZoo) to test the outcomes of machine learning techniques. Other vendors offer added value by repackaging open source tools in a simpler way and bringing the tools to market.

Vendors such as Cloudera, Hortonworks, and Pivotal have provided this value-add for the open source framework Hadoop.

As the new ecosystem takes shape, there are four main groups of players within this interconnected web.

- Data devices and the "Sensornet" gat her data from multiple locations and continuously generate new data about this data. For each gigabyte of new data created, an additional petabyte of data is created about that data.

- For example, consider someone playing an online video game through a PC, game console, or smartphone. In this case, the video game provider captures data about the skill and levels attained by the player. Intelligent systems monitor and log how and when the user plays the game. As a consequence, the game provider can fine-tune the difficulty of the game, suggest other related games that would most likely interest the user, and offer additional equipment and enhancements for the character based on the user's age, gender, and interests. This information may get stored locally or uploaded to the game provider's cloud to analyze the gaming habits and opportunities for ups ell and cross-sell, and identify archetypical profiles of specific kinds of users.

- Smartphones provide another rich source of data. In addition to messaging and basic phone usage, they store and transmit data about Internet usage, SMS usage, and real-time location. This metadata can be used for analyzing traffic patterns by scanning the density of smartphones in locations to track the speed of cars or the relative traffic congestion on busy roads. In this way, GPS devices in cars can give drivers real-time updates and offer alternative routes to avoid traffic delays.

• Retail shopping loyalty cards record not just the amount an individual spends, but the locations of stores that person visits, the kinds of products purchased, the stores where goods are purchased most often, and the combinations of products purchased together. Collecting this data provides insights into shopping and travel habits and the likelihood of successful advertisement targeting for certain types of retail promotions.

• Data collectors include sample entities that collect data from the device and users.

• Data results from a cable TV provider tracking the shows a person watches, which TV channels someone wi ll and will not pay for to watch on demand, and the prices someone is willing to pay for premium TV content

• Retail stores tracking the path a customer takes through their store while pushing a shopping cart with an RFID chip so they can gauge which products get the most foot traffic using geospatial data collected from the RFID chips

- Data aggregators make sense of the data collected from the various entities from the "SensorNet" or the "Internet ofThings." These organizations compile data from the devices and usage patterns collected by government agencies, retail stores, and websites. In turn, they can choose to transform and package the data as products to sell to list brokers, who may want to generate marketing lists of people who may be good targets for specific ad campaigns.

- Retail banks, acting as a data buyer, may want to know which customers have the highest likelihood to apply for a second mortgage or a home equity line of credit. To provide input for this analysis, retail banks may purchase data from a data aggregator. This kind of data may include demographic information about people living in specific locations; people who appear to have a specific level of debt, yet still have solid credit scores (or other characteristics such as paying bills on time and having savings accounts) that can be used to infer credit worthiness; and those who are searching the web for information about paying off debts or doing home remodeling projects. Obtaining data from these various sources and aggregators will enable a more targeted marketing campaign, which would have been more challenging before Big Data due to the lack of information or high-performing technologies.

•   Using technologies such as Hadoop to perform natural language processing on unstructured, textual data from social media websites, users can gauge the reaction to events such as presidential campaigns. People may, for example, want to determine public sentiments toward a candidate by analyzing related blogs and online comments. Similarly, data users may want to track and prepare for natural disasters by identifying which areas a hurricane affects first and how it moves, based on which geographic areas are tweeting about it or discussing it via social media.

As illustrated by this emerging Big Data ecosystem, the kinds of data and the related market dynamics vary greatly. These data sets can include sensor data, text, structured datasets, and social media. With this in mind, it is worth recalling that these data sets will not work well within traditional EDWs, which were architected to streamline reporting and dashboards and be centrally managed.Instead, Big Data problems and projects require different approaches to succeed.

Analysts need to partner with IT and DBAs to get the data they need within an analytic sandbox. A typical analytical sandbox contains raw data, aggregated data, and data with multiple kinds of structure.

The sandbox enables robust exploration of data and requires a savvy user to leverage and take advantage of data in the sandbox environment.

CHAPTER 7

Text Mining And Text Analytics

Most of the human recorded information in the world is in the form of written text. We all learn to read and write from infancy so we can express ourselves through writing and learn what others know, think, and feel. We use this skill all the time when reading or writing an email, a blog, text messages, or this book, so it's no wonder written language comes naturally to most of us. Businesses are convinced that much value can be found in the texts that people produce, and rightly so because they contain information on what those people like, dislike, what they know or would like to know, crave and desire, their current health or mood, and so much more. Many of these things can be relevant for companies or researchers, but no single person can read and interpret this tsunami of written material by themself. Once again, we need to turn to computers to do the job for us.

Sadly, however, the natural language doesn't come as "natural" to computers as it does to humans. Deriving meaning and filtering out the unimportant from the important is still something a human is better at than any machine. Luckily, data scientists can apply specific text mining and text analytics techniques to find the relevant information in heaps of text that would otherwise take them centuries to read themselves.

Text mining or text analytics is a discipline that combines language science and computer science with statistical and machine learning techniques. Text mining is used for analyzing texts and turning them into a more structured form. Then it takes this structured form and tries to derive insights from it. When analyzing crime from police reports, for example, text mining helps you recognize persons, places, and types of crimes from the reports. Then this new structure is used to gain insight into the evolution of crimes.

While language isn't limited to the natural language, the focus of this chapter will be on Natural Language Processing (NLP). Examples of non-natural languages would be machine logs, mathematics, and Morse code. Technically even Esperanto, Klingon, and Dragon language aren't in the field of natural languages because they were invented deliberately instead of evolving over time; they didn't come "natural" to us.

These last languages are nevertheless fit for natural communication (speech, writing); they have a grammar and a vocabulary as all natural languages do, and the same text mining techniques could apply to them.

Text mining in the real world

In your day-to-day life you've already come across text mining and natural language applications. Autocomplete and spelling correctors are constantly analyzing the text you type before sending an email or text message. When Facebook autocompletes your status with the name of a friend, it does this with the help of a technique called named entity recognition, although this would be only one component of their repertoire.

The goal isn't only to detect that you're typing a noun, but also to guess you're referring to a person and recognize who it might be. Another example of named entity recognition. Google knows Chelsea is a football club but responds differently when asked for a person.

Google uses many types of text mining when presenting you with the results of a query. What pops up in your own mind when someone says

"Chelsea"? Chelsea could be many things: a person; a soccer club; a neighborhood in Manhattan, New York or London; a food market; a flower show; and so on. Google knows this and returns different answers to the question "Who is Chelsea?" versus "What is Chelsea?"

To provide the most relevant answer, Google must do (among other things) all of the following:

- Preprocess all the documents it collects for named entities

- Perform language identification

- Detect what type of entity you're referring to

- Match a query to a result

- Detect the type of content to return (PDF, adult-sensitive)

This example shows that text mining isn't only about the direct meaning of text itself but also involves meta-attributes such as language and document type.

Google uses text mining for much more than answering queries. Next to shielding its Gmail users from spam, it also divides the emails into different categories such as social, updates, and forums. It's possible to go much further than answering simple questions when you combine text with other logic and mathematics.

If this isn't impressive enough, the IBM Watson astonished many in 2011 when the machine was set up against two human players in a game of Jeopardy. Jeopardy is an American quiz show where people receive the answer to a question and points are scored for guessing the correct question for that answer.

It's safe to say this round goes to artificial intelligence. IBM Watson is a cognitive engine that can interpret natural language and answer questions based on an extensive knowledge base.

Text mining has many applications, including, but not limited to, the following:

- Entity identification

- Plagiarism detection

- Topic identification

- Text clustering

- Translation

- Automatic text summarization

- Fraud detection

- Spam filtering

- Sentiment analysis

Text mining is useful, but is it difficult? Sorry to disappoint: Yes, it is.

When looking at the examples of Wolfram Alpha and IBM Watson, you might have gotten the impression that text mining is easy. Sadly, no. In reality text mining is a complicated task and even many seemingly simple things can't be done satisfactorily.

For instance, take the task of guessing the correct address. Its shows how difficult it is to return the exact result with certitude and how Google Maps prompts you for more information when looking for "Springfield." In this case a human wouldn't have done any better without additional context, but this ambiguity is one of the many problems you face in a text mining application.

Another problem is spelling mistakes and different (correct) spelling forms of a word. Take the following three references to New York: "NY," "Neww York," and "New York." For a human, it's easy to see they all refer to the city of New York. Because of the way our brain interprets text, understanding text with spelling mistakes comes naturally to us; people may not even notice them. But for a computer these are unrelated strings unless we use algorithms to tell it that they're referring to the same entity. Related problems are synonyms and the use of pronouns. Try assigning the right person to the pronoun "she" in the next sentences: "John gave flowers to Marleen's parents when he met her parents for the first time. She was so happy with this gesture." Easy enough, right? Not for a computer.

We can solve many similar problems with ease, but they often prove hard for a machine. We can train algorithms that work well on a specific problem in a welldefined scope, but more general algorithms that work in all cases are another beast altogether. For instance, we can teach a computer to recognize and retrieve US account numbers from text, but this doesn't generalize well to account numbers from other countries.

Language algorithms are also sensitive to the context the language is used in, even if the language itself remains the same. English models won't work for Arabic and vice versa, but even if we keep to English — an algorithm trained for Twitter data isn't likely to perform well on legal texts. Let's keep this in mind when we move on to the chapter case study: there's no perfect, one-size-fits-all solution in text mining.

Text mining techniques

During our upcoming case study we'll tackle the problem of text classification: automatically classifying uncategorized texts into specific categories. To get from raw textual data to our final destination we'll need a few data mining techniques that require background information for us to use them effectively. The first important concept in text mining is the "bag of words."

Bag of words

To build our classification model we'll go with the bag of words approach. Bag of words is the simplest way of structuring textual data: every document is turned into a word vector. If a certain word is present in the vector it's labeled "True"; the others

are labeled "False". in case there are only two documents: one about the television show Game of Thrones and one about data science. The two word vectors together form the document-term matrix. The document-term matrix holds a column for every term and a row for every document. The values are yours to decide upon. In this chapter we'll use binary: term is present? True or False.

A big corpus can have thousands of unique words. If all have to be labeled like this without any filtering, it's easy to see we might end up with a large volume of data. Binary coded bag of words is but one way to structure the data; other techniques exist.

Before getting to the actual bag of words, many other data manipulation steps take place:

Tokenization—The text is cut into pieces called "tokens" or "terms." These tokens are the most basic unit of information you'll use for your model. The terms are often words but this isn't a necessity. Entire sentences can be used for analysis. We'll use unigrams: terms consisting of one word. Often, however, it's useful to include bigrams (two words per token) or trigrams (three words per token) to capture extra meaning and increase the performance of your models.

This does come at a cost, though, because you're building bigger term-vectors by including bigrams and/or trigrams in the equation.

Stop word filtering—Every language comes with words that have little value in text analytics because they're used so often. NLTK comes with a short list of English stop words we can filter. If the text is tokenized into words, it often makes sense to rid the word vector of these low-information stop words.

Lowercasing—Words with capital letters appear at the beginning of a sentence, others because they're proper nouns or adjectives. We gain no added value making that distinction in our term matrix, so all terms will be set to lowercase. Another data preparation technique is stemming. This one requires more elaboration.

Stemming and lemmatization

Stemming is the process of bringing words back to their root form; this way you end up with less variance in the data. This makes sense if words have similar meanings but are written differently because, for example, one is in its plural form. Stemming attempts to unify by cutting off parts of the word. For example "planes" and "plane" both become "plane."

Another technique, called lemmatization, has this same goal but does so in a more grammatically sensitive way. For example, while both stemming and lemmatization would reduce "cars" to "car," lemmatization can also bring back conjugated verbs to their unconjugated forms such as "are" to "be." Which one you use depends on your case, and lemmatization profits heavily from POS Tagging (Part of Speech Tagging).

POS Tagging is the process of attributing a grammatical label to every part of a sentence. You probably did this manually in school as a language exercise. Take the sentence "Game of Thrones is a television series." If we apply   POS   Tagging   on   it   we   get

({"game":"NN"},{"of":"IN},{"thrones":"NNS},{"is":"VBZ},{"a":"DT},{"telev ision":"NN},

{"series":"NN}) NN is a noun, IN is a preposition, NNS is a noun in its plural form, VBZ is a third-person singular verb, and DT is a determiner.

POS Tagging is a use case of sentence-tokenization rather than word-tokenization.

After the POS Tagging is complete you can still proceed to word tokenization, but a POS Tagger requires whole sentences. Combining POS Tagging and lemmatization is likely to give cleaner data than using only a stemmer. For the sake of simplicity we'll stick to stemming in the case study, but consider this an opportunity to elaborate on the exercise.

We now know the most important things we'll use to do the data cleansing and manipulation (text mining). For our text analytics, let's add the decision tree classifier to our repertoire.

Decision tree classifier

The data analysis part of our case study will be kept simple as well. We'll test a Naïve Bayes classifier and a decision tree classifier. As seen in chapter 3 the Naïve Bayes classifier is called that because it considers each input variable to be independent of all the others, which is naïve, especially in text mining. Take the simple examples of "data science," "data analysis," or "game of thrones." If we cut our data in unigrams we get the following separate variables (if we ignore stemming and such): "data," "science," "analysis," "game," "of," and "thrones." Obviously links will be lost. This can, in turn, be overcome by creating bigrams (data science, data analysis) and trigrams (game of thrones).

The decision tree classifier, however, doesn't consider the variables to be independent of one another and actively creates interaction variables and buckets. An interaction variable is a variable that combines other variables. For instance "data" and "science" might be good predictors in their own right but probably the two of them co-occurring in the same text might have its own value. A bucket is somewhat the opposite. Instead of combining two variables, a variable is split into multiple new ones. This makes sense for numerical variables.

Whereas Naïve Bayes supposes independence of all the input variables, a decision tree is built upon the assumption of interdependence. But how does it build this structure? A decision tree has a few possible criteria it can use to split into branches and decide which variables are more important (are closer to the root of the tree) than others. The one we'll use in the NLTK decision tree classifier is "information gain." To understand information gain, we first need to look at entropy. Entropy is a measure of unpredictability or chaos. A simple example would be the gender of a baby. When a woman is pregnant, the gender of the fetus can be male or female, but we don't know which one it is. If you were to guess, you have a 50% chance to guess correctly (give or take, because gender distribution isn't 100% uniform). However, during the pregnancy you have the opportunity to do an ultrasound to determine the gender of the fetus. An ultrasound is never 100% conclusive, but the farther along in fetal development, the more accurate it becomes. This accuracy gain, or information gain, is there because uncertainty or entropy drops. Let's say an ultrasound at 12 weeks pregnancy has a 90% accuracy in determining the gender of the baby. A 10% uncertainty still exists, but the ultrasound did reduce the uncertainty from 50% to 10%. That's a pretty good discriminator. A decision tree follows this same principle.

If another gender test has more predictive power, it could become the root of the tree with the ultrasound test being in the branches, and this can go on until we run out of variables or observations. We can run out of observations, because at every branch split we also split the input data. This is a big weakness of the decision tree, because at the leaf level of the tree robustness breaks down if too few observations are left; the decision trees starts to overfit the data. Overfitting allows the model to mistake randomness for real correlations. To counteract this, a decision tree is pruned: its meaningless branches are left out of the final model.

CHAPTER 8

Data Visualization

You have several options for delivering a dashboard to your end users. Here we'll focus on a single option, and by the end of this chapter you'll be able to create a dashboard yourself.

This chapter's case is that of a hospital pharmacy with a stock of a few thousand medicines. The government came out with a new norm to all pharmacies: all medicines should be checked for their sensitivity to light and be stored in new, special containers.

One thing the government didn't supply to the pharmacies was an actual list of light-sensitive medicines. This is no problem for you as a data scientist because every medicine has a patient information leaflet that contains this information. You distill the information with the clever use of text mining and assign a "light sensitive" or "not light sensitive" tag to each medicine. This information is then uploaded to the central database.

In addition, the pharmacy needs to know how many containers would be necessary. For this they give you access to the pharmacy stock data. When you draw a sample with only the variables you require.

As you can see, the information is time-series data for an entire year of stock movement, so every medicine thus has 365 entries in the data set. Although the case study is an existing one and the medicines in the data set are real, the values of the other variables presented here were randomly generated, as the original data is classified. Also, the data set is limited to 29 medicines, a little more than 10,000 lines of data. Even though people do create reports using crossfilter.js (a Javascript MapReduce library) and dc.js (a Javascript dashboarding library) with more than a million lines of data, for the example's sake you'll use a fraction of this amount. Also, it's not recommended to load your entire database into the user's browser; the browser will freeze while loading, and if it's too much data, the browser will even crash. Normally data is precalculated on the server and parts of it are requested using, for example, a REST service. To turn this data into an actual dashboard you have many options.

Among all the options, for this book we decided to go with dc.js, which is a crossbreed between the JavaScript MapReduce library Crossfilter and the data visualization library d3.js. Crossfilter was developed by Square Register, a company that handles payment transactions; it's comparable to PayPal but its focus is on mobile. Square developed Crossfilter to allow their customers extremely speedy slice and dice on their payment history. Crossfilter is not the only JavaScript library capable of MapReduce processing, but it most certainly does the job, is open source, is free to use, and is maintained by an established company (Square). Example alternatives to Crossfilter are Map.js, Meguro, and Underscore.js. JavaScript might not be known as a data crunching language, but these libraries do give web browsers that extra bit of punch in case data does need to be handled in the browser. We won't go into how JavaScript can be used for massive calculations within collaborative distributed frameworks, but an army of dwarfs can topple a giant. If this topic interests you, you can read more about it at https://www.igvita.com/2009/03/03/collaborative-map-reducein-the-browser/ and at http://dyn.com/blog/browsers-vs-servers-using-javascript-fornumber-crunching-theories/. d3.js can safely be called the most versatile JavaScript data visualization library available at the time of writing; it was developed by Mike Bostock as a successor to his Protovis library. Many JavaScript libraries are built on top of d3.js.

NVD3, C3.js, xCharts, and Dimple offer roughly the same thing: an abstraction layer on top of d3.js, which makes it easier to draw simple graphs. They mainly differ in the type of graphs they support and their default design. Feel free to visit their websites and find out for yourself:

- *NVD3 – http://nvd3.org/*

- *C3.js – http://c3js.org/*

- *xCharts – http://tenxer.github.io/xcharts/*

- *Dimple – http://dimplejs.org/*

Many options exist. So why dc.js?

The main reason: compared to what it delivers, an interactive dashboard where clicking one graph will create filtered views on related graphs, dc.js is surprisingly easy to set up. It's so easy that you'll have a working example by the end of this chapter. As a data scientist, you already put in enough time on your actual analysis; easy-to-implement dashboards are a welcome gift.

To get an idea of what you're about to create, you can go to the following website, http://dc-js.github.io/dc.js/, and scroll down to the NASDAQ example.

Click around the dashboard and see the graphs react and interact when you select and deselect data points. Don't spend too long though; it's time to create this yourself.

As stated before, dc.js has two big prerequisites: d3.js and crossfilter.js. d3.js has a steep learning curve and there are several books on the topic worth reading if you're interested in full customization of your visualizations. But to work with dc.js, no knowledge of it is required, so we won't go into it in this book. Crossfilter.js is another matter; you'll need to have a little grasp of this MapReduce library to get dc.js up and running on your data. But because the concept of MapReduce itself isn't new, this will go smoothly.

Crossfilter, the JavaScript MapReduce library

JavaScript isn't the greatest language for data crunching. But that didn't stop people, like the folks at Square, from developing MapReduce libraries for it. If you're dealing with data, every bit of speed gain helps. You don't want to send enormous loads of data over the internet or even your internal network though, for these reasons:

•   Sending a bulk of data will tax the network to the point where it will bother other users.

•   The browser is on the receiving end, and while loading in the data it will temporarily freeze. For small amounts of data this is unnoticeable, but when you start looking at 100,000 lines, it can become a visible lag. When you go over 1,000,000 lines, depending on the width of your data, your browser could give up on you.

it's a balance exercise. For the data you do send, there is a Crossfilter to handle it for you once it arrives in the browser. In our case study, the pharmacist requested the central server for stock data of 2015 for 29 medicines she was particularly interested in. We already took a look at the data, so let's dive into the application itself.

Setting up everything

It's time to build the actual application, and the ingredients of our small dc.js application are as follows:

JQuery — *To handle the interactivity*

Crossfilter.js — *A MapReduce library and prerequisite to dc.js*

d3.js — *A popular data visualization library and prerequisite to dc.js*

dc.js — *The visualization library you will use to create your interactive dashboard*

Bootstrap — *A widely used layout library you'll use to make it all look better*

You'll write only three files:

index.html — *The HTML page that contains your application*

application.js — *To hold all the JavaScript code you'll write*

application.css — *For your own CSS*

In addition, you'll need to run our code on an HTTP server. You could go through the effort of setting up a LAMP (Linux, Apache, MySQL, PHP), WAMP (Windows, Apache, MySQL, PHP), or XAMPP (Cross Environment, Apache, MySQL, PHP, Perl) server. But for the sake of simplicity we won't set up any of those servers here. Instead you can do it with a single Python command. Use your command-line tool (Linux shell or Windows CMD) and move to the folder containing your index.html (once it's there). You should have Python installed for other chapters of this book so the following command should launch a Python HTTP server on your localhost. python -m SimpleHTTPServer

For Python 3.4

python -m http.server 8000

An HTTP server is started on localhost port 8000. In your browser this translates to "localhost:8000"; putting "0.0.0.0:8000" won't work.

Make sure to have all the required files available in the same folder as your index.html.

You can download them from the Manning website or from their creators' websites.

- *dc.css and dc.min.js – https://dc-js.github.io/dc.js/*

- *d3.v3.min.js – http://d3js.org/*

- *crossfilter.min.js – http://square.github.io/crossfilter/*

Now we know how to run the code we're about to create, so let's look at the index.html page.

No surprises here. The header contains all the CSS libraries you'll use, so we'll load our JavaScript at the end of the HTML body. Using a JQuery onload handler, your application will be loaded when the rest of the page is ready. You start off with two table placeholders: one to show what your input data looks like, <div id="inputtable"></div>, and the other one will be used with Crossfilter to show a filtered table, <div id="filteredtable"></div>. Several Bootstrap CSS classes were used, such as "well", "container", the Bootstrap grid system with "row" and "col-xx-xx", and so on. They make the whole thing look nicer but they aren't mandatory. More information on the Bootstrap CSS classes can be found on their website at http://getbootstrap.com/css/.

Now that you have your HTML set up, it's time to show your data onscreen. For this, turn your attention to the application.js file you created. First, we wrap the entire code "to be" in a JQuery onload handler.

$(function() {

```
//All future code will end up in this wrapper
```

```
})
```

Now we're certain our application will be loaded only when all else is ready. This is important because we'll use JQuery selectors to manipulate the HTML. It's time to load in data.

```
d3.csv('medicines.csv',function(data) {
```

```
main(data)
```

```
});
```

You don't have a REST service ready and waiting for you, so for the example you'll draw the data from a .csv file. This file is available for download on Manning's website. d3.js offers an easy function for that. After loading in the data you hand it over to your main application function in the d3.csv callback function.

Unleashing Crossfilter to filter the medicine data set

Now let's go into Crossfilter to use filtering and MapReduce. Henceforth you can put all the upcoming code after the code of section 9.2.1 within the main() function.

The first thing you'll need to do is declare a Crossfilter instance and initiate it with your data.

CrossfilterInstance = crossfilter(medicineData);

From here you can get to work. On this instance you can register dimensions, which are the columns of your table. Currently Crossfilter is limited to 32 dimensions. If you're handling data wider than 32 dimensions, you should consider narrowing it down before sending it to the browser. Let's create our first dimension, the medicine name dimension:

var medNameDim = CrossfilterInstance.dimension(function(d) {return

d.MedName;});

Your first dimension is the name of the medicines, and you can already use this to filter your data set and show the filtered data using our CreateTable() function.

- *var dataFiltered= medNameDim.filter('Grazax 75 000 SQ-T')*

- *var filteredTable = $('#filteredtable');*

- *filteredTable*

- *.empty().append(CreateTable(dataFiltered.top(5),variablesInTable,'Our*

- *First Filtered Table'));*

You show only the top five observations; you have 365 because you have the results from a single medicine for an entire year.

CHAPTER 9

Appendix A - Setting Up Elasticsearch

Linux installation

First check to see if you have Java already installed on your machine.

1) You can check your Java version in a console window with java – version. If Java is installed. You'll need at least Java 7 to run the version of Elasticsearch we use in this book. Note: Elasticsearch had moved on to version 2 by the time this book was released, but while code might change slightly, the core principles remain the same.

2) If Java isn't installed or you don't have a high enough version, Elasticsearch recommends the Oracle version of Java. Use the following console commands to install it.

sudo add-apt-repository ppa:webupd8team/java sudo apt-get install oracle-java7-installer

Now you can install Elasticsearch:

1) Add the Elasticsearch 1.4 repo, which is the latest one at the time of writing, to your repo list and then install it with the following commands.

sudo add-apt-repository "deb http://packages.Elasticsearch.org/ ➡ Elasticsearch/1.4/debian stable main" sudo apt-get update && sudo apt-get install Elasticsearch

2) To make sure Elasticsearch will start on reboot, run the following command. sudo update-rc.d Elasticsearch defaults 95 10

3) Turn on Elasticsearch.

sudo /etc/init.d/Elasticsearch start

If Linux is your local computer, open a browser and go to localhost:9200. 9200 is the default port for the Elasticsearch API.

The Elasticsearch welcome screen should greet you. Notice your database even has a name. The name is picked from the pool of Marvel characters and changes every time you reboot your database. In production, having an inconsistent and non-unique name such as this can be problematic. The instance you started is a single node of what could be part of a huge distributed cluster. If all of these nodes change names on reboot, it becomes nearly impossible to track them with logs in case of trouble. Elasticsearch takes pride in the fact it has little need for configuration to get you started and is distributed by nature. While this is most certainly true, things such as this random name prove that deploying an actual multi-node setup will require you to think twice about certain default settings. Luckily Elasticsearch has adequate documentation on almost everything, including deployment

(http://www.Elasticsearch.org/guide/en/Elasticsearch/guide/current/d eploy.html). Multi-node Elasticsearch deployment isn't in the scope of this chapter but it's good to keep in mind.

Windows installation

InWindows, Elasticsearch also requires at least Java 7—the JRE and the JDK—to be installed and for the JAVA_HOME variable to be pointing at the Java folder.

1} Download the Windows installers for Java from http://www.oracle.com/technetwork/java/javase/downloads/index.html and run them.

2} After installation make sure your JAVA_HOME Windows environment variable points to where you installed the Java Development Kit. You can find your environment variables in System Control Panel > Advanced System Settings. Attempting an install before you have an adequate Java version will result in an error.

Installing on a PC with limited rights

Sometimes you want to try a piece of software but you aren't free to install your own programs. If that's the case, don't despair: portable JDKs are out there. When you find one of those you can temporarily set your JAVA_HOME variable to the path of the portable JDK and start Elasticsearch this way. You don't even need to install Elasticsearch if you're only checking it out.

Now that you have Java installed and set up, you can install Elasticsearch.

1} Download the Elasticsearch zip package manually from http://www.Elasticsearch.org/download/. Unpack it anywhere on your computer. This folder will now become your self-contained database. If you have an SSD drive, consider giving it a place there, because it significantly increases the speed of Elasticsearch.

2} If you already have a Windows command window open, don't use it for the installation; open a fresh one instead. The environment variables in the open window aren't up to date anymore. Change the directory to your Elasticsearch /bin folder and install using the service install command.

3} The database should now be ready to start. Use the service start command.

If you want to stop the server, issue the service stop command. Open your browser of choice and put localhost:9200 in the address bar. If the Elasticsearch welcome screen appears, you've successfully installed Elasticsearch.

CHAPTER 10

Linux installation

To install Neo4j community edition on Linux, use your command line as instructed   here: http://debian.neo4j.org/?_ga=1.84149595.332593114.1442594242.

 Neo Technology provides this Debian repository to make it easy to install Neo4j.

It includes three repositories:

Stable — All Neo4j releases, except as noted below. You should choose this by default.

Testing — Pre-release versions (milestones and release candidates).

Oldstable — No longer actively used, this repository contains patch releases for old minor versions. If you can't find what you need in Stable, then look here.

To use the new Stable packages, you need to run the commands below as root (note that we use sudo below):

sudo -s

wget -O - https://debian.neo4j.org/neotechnology.gpg.key | apt-key add - #

Import our signing key

echo 'deb http://debian.neo4j.org/repo stable/' > /etc/apt/sources.list.d/

neo4j.list # Create an Apt sources.list file

aptitude update -y # Find out about the files in our repository

aptitude install neo4j -y # Install Neo4j, community edition

You could replace Stable with Testing if you want a newer (but unsupported) build of Neo4j. If you'd like a different edition, you can run:

apt-get install neo4j-advanced or

apt-get install neo4j-enterprise

Windows installation

To install the Neo4j community edition on Windows:

1} Go to http://neo4j.com/download/ and download the community edition. Thefollowing screen will appear.

2} Save this file and run it.

3} After installation, you'll get a new pop up that gives you the option to choose the default database location or alternatively browse to find another location to use as the database location.

4} After making your choice, press Start and you're ready to go. In a few seconds, the database will be ready to use. If you want to stop the server you can just press the Stop button.

5} Open your browser of choice and put localhost:7474 in the address bar. You have arrived at the Neo4j browser.

6} When the database access asks for authentication, use the username and password "neo4j", then press Connect.

In the following window you can set your own password.

Now you can input your Cypher queries and consult your nodes, relationships, and results.

appendix C - Installing MySQL server

Windows installation

The most convenient and recommended method is to download MySQL installer (for Windows) and let it set up all of the MySQL components on your system. The following steps explain how to do it:

1} Download MySQL Installer from http://dev.mysql.com/downloads/installer/ and open it. Please notice that, unlike the standard MySQL installer, the smaller "web-group" version does automatically include any MySQL components, but will only download the ones you choose to install. Feel free to pick either installer.

2} Select the suitable Setup Type you prefer. The option Developer Default will install MySQL server and other MySQL components related to MySQL advancement, together with supportive functions such as MySQL Workbench. You can also choose Custom Setup if you want to select the

MySQL items that will be installed on your system. And you can always have different versions of MySQL operate on a single system, if you wish. The MySQL notifier is useful for monitoring the running instances, stopping them, and restarting them. You can also add this later using the MySQL installer.

3} Then the MySQL installation wizard's instructions will guide you through the setup process. It's mostly accepting what's to come. A development machine will do as the server configuration type. Make sure to set a MySQL root password and don't forget what it is, because you need it later. You can run it as a Windows service; that way, you don't need to launch it manually.

4} The installation completes. If you opted for a full install, by default MySQL server, MySQL workbench, and MySQL notifier will start automatically at computer startup. MySQL installer can be used to upgrade or change settings of installed components.

5} The instance should be up and running, and you can connect to it using the MySQL workbench.

Linux installation

The official installation instructions for MySQL on Linux can be found at https:// dev.mysql.com/doc/refman/5.7/en/linux-installation.html.

However, certain Linux distributions give specific installation guides for it. For example, the instructions for installing Linux on Ubuntu 14.04 can be found at

https://www.linode.com/docs/databases/mysql/how-to-install-mysql-on-ubuntu-14-04.

The following instructions are based on the official instructions.

1) First check your hostname:

hostname

hostname -f

The first command should show your short hostname, and the second should show your fully qualified domain name (FQDN).

2) Update your system:

sudo apt-get update

sudo apt-get upgrade

3 Install MySQL:

Sudo apt-get install msql-server

During the installation process, you'll get a message to choose a password for the MySQL root user.

MySQL will bind to localhost (127.0.0.1) by default.

4 Log into MySQL:

mysql –u root –p

Enter the password you chose and you should see the MySQL console.

5 Finally, create a schema so you have something to refer to .

Create database test;

Appendix D

Setting up Anaconda with a virtual environment

Anaconda is a Python code package that's especially useful for data science. The default installation will have many tools a data scientist might use. In this book we'll use the 32-bit version because it often remains more stable with many Python packages (especially the SQL ones).

While we recommend using Anaconda, this is in no way required. In this appendix, we'll cover installing and setting up Anaconda. Instructions for Linux and Windows installations are included, followed by environment setup instructions. If you know a thing or two about using Python packages, feel free to do it your own way. For instance, you could use virtualenv and pip libraries.

Linux installation

To install Anaconda on Linux:

1} Go to https://www.continuum.io/downloads and download the Linux installer for the 32-bit version of Anaconda based on Python 2.7.

2} When the download is done use the following command to install Anaconda: bash Anaconda2-2.4.0-Linux-x86_64.sh

3} We need to get the conda command working in the Linux command prompt. Anaconda will ask you whether it needs to do that, so answer "yes".

Windows installation

To install Anaconda on Windows:

1} Go to https://www.continuum.io/downloads and download the Windows installer for the 32-bit version of Anaconda based on Python 2.7.

2} Run the installer.

Setting up the environment

Once the installation is done, it's time to set up an environment. An interesting schema on conda vs pip commands can be found at http://conda.pydata.org/docs/ _downloads/conda-pip-virtualenv-translator.html.

1} Use the following command in your operating system command line. Replace "nameoftheenv" with the actual name you want your environment to have. conda create –n name of the environment anaconda

2} Make sure you agree to proceed with the setup by typing "y" at the end of this list, as shown in figure D.1, and after awhile you should be ready to go. Anaconda will create the environment on its default location, but options are available if you want to change the location.

3} Now that you have an environment, you can activate it in the command line:

– In Windows, type activate nameoftheenv

– In Linux, type source activate nameoftheenv

Or you can point to it with your Python IDE (integrated development environment).

4} If you activate it in the command line you can start up the Jupiter (or IPython) IDE with the following command:

Ipython notebook

Jupiter (formerly known as IPython) is an interactive Python development interface that runs in the browser. It's useful for adding structure to your code.

5} For every package mentioned in the book that isn't installed in the default Anaconda environment:

a) Activate your environment in the command line.

B) Either use conda install libraryname or pip install libraryname in the command line.

For more information on the pip install, visit http://python-packaging-userguide.readthedocs.org/en/latest/installing/.

For more information on the Anaconda conda install, visit http://conda.pydata .org/docs/intro.html.

Thank you for reading this book!

www.ingramcontent.com/pod-product-compliance
Lightning Source LLC
Chambersburg PA
CBHW071216220526
45468CB00002B/633